The Best Cook

by Anne Walsh
illustrated by Kersti Frigell

Practice Decodable 74

McGraw Hill Education

Bothell, WA • Chicago, IL • Columbus, OH • New York, NY

MHEonline.com

Send all inquiries to:
McGraw-Hill Education
8787 Orion Place
Columbus, OH 43240

ISBN: 978-0-02-144978-1
MHID: 0-02-144978-3

Printed in China.

8 9 10 11 12 DSS 27 26 25 24 23

My mom is a good cook. She makes tasty meals. My dad is a better cook.

Mom traveled all over to study cooking. She took cooking lessons for weeks.

Dad never took cooking lessons. He has cooked all his life. He learned from his family.

Mom keeps lots of cookbooks on a wooden bookcase. She looks at them for ideas.

Dad uses cookbooks a little. Yesterday, he stood on a cookbook to get a pan.

Mom and Dad share cooking tips. Mom is a good cook, but Dad is the best.